Bigfoot Field Work 101

Volume two: Choosing a Research Area

William Jevning

Copyright © 2015 William Jevning

All rights reserved.

ISBN: 10: 1519796714
ISBN-13: 978-1519796714

DEDICATION

To all who seek adventure and knowledge

ACKNOWLEDGMENTS

I wish to thank all those who have helped me along my journey. I have had the great fortune to have known and shared friendships with so many wonderful people during my years of work in this topic.

If you have the equipment I recommended in volume one, you are ready for the next step in conducting Bigfoot field work. Now you must choose where you wish to start searching, and this can be a daunting task. . In today's world of fast communications, and social media, the topic of Bigfoot has been gaining general acceptance and this newfound popularity of the subject has seen a flood of new self-described experts.

Anyone making the decision to enter this field can become very confused at best, and downright overwhelmed by all the information available. There are conflicting views and opinions by many claiming expertise, so I am suggesting that you start with a clean slate.

There is a Rene' Dahinden quote that is a favorite of mine, and it is correct for this and generally any topic of research. Rene was quoted as saying:

"If information and knowledge is not shared and received through integrity, hard work, cooperation, and dedication, we achieve nothing, and the unknown may forever remain so."

"Everyone has a right to their own opinion, but no one has a right to be wrong about the Facts. Without the facts, your opinion is of no value."
    Rene' Dahinden.

What he said is a truth most today either ignore or have forgotten, but it is correct. Because there has been so much information regarding the Sasquatch on the internet, television, radio, podcasts, blogs and websites for anyone entering this field, I suggest never relying on any of these sources. To choose an area to begin your field work there are some basics concepts that will provide great value.

You may rightly ask then, just where to begin? In today's information society it is very easy to simply do internet searches, and while these do have their value, there is no substitute for old fashioned footwork.

Something I learned in my first couple years of college, while studying archaeology, was finding a site to research. In searching for early or historical human dwelling locations we first had to know something about the habits of the people we were searching for. For instance; the places where Native people would make hunting or fishing camps generally were near two streams of water joined together; we were even given the term project of trying to locate such a place and generally this method worked well.

The point is doing research of activity, in a particular area should be your first step, and there are some good resources to utilize for this. There are websites that list sightings in locations around the country and elsewhere, but most often these are not firsthand accounts. Often times, witness accounts are copied many times over and the problem with this is they can be altered as they get re-copied.

For purposes of having as accurate information as possible, you should attempt to track down original sources. You should try to research as far back into an area as possible, old newspaper articles are an excellent place to begin. There are newspaper articles that date back to the early 1800's, about people encountering hairy wild men, and there are good details that may aid you in establishing a foundation for the area you choose.

If you choose an area that does not have much of a historical record of the creatures being encountered, you may wish to look elsewhere. In my early days of involvement into the topic of Bigfoot, I was told by several of the original pioneers of the subject that what they had learned was that the Sasquatch was not evenly distributed around the country, but was in specific locations.

That was somewhat true of the late 1950's through the mid 1970's as the population has no doubt grown since then and human activities have caused them to move to places they may not previously have been, however searching historical records will provide you with a solid foundation of where to begin looking.

As I had mentioned, collecting old newspaper stories is one excellent place to start, local libraries contain archived newspaper stories. Contacting a local library is a place you will find books about the topic, but more importantly old articles. Often in older articles especially names of witnesses, locations and photographs are contained and can be very useful. By collecting as many articles, magazine articles related to witness accounts to a given region and journal entries by mountain men, adventurers and early explorers will not only provide you with a foundation but movement patterns of the creatures.

On the following page is an example of one such article from 1975, this incident occurred just a few miles from where I had my own encounter with two Sasquatches just a year earlier. There were other articles as people came forward in that area back then, however most witnesses did not tell what they had seen and this is true in most places but these types of articles are a big help. Notice the hand writing at the top of the article, libraries may categorize newspaper clippings into various categories so you may have to be creative in your queries.

Hunters find smaller set of mystery footprints

By KERRY WEBSTER
TNT Staff Writer

PUYALLUP — Two raccoon hunters who found a set of huge footprints near here last week now claim to have discovered another trail in the same area.

Mel Groove, 24, of 2802 Alder Ct. N., and Robert Beckham Jr., of 3838 E. I St., Tacoma, said Tuesday they found another, slightly smaller set of footprints in a wooded area near the Forest Green housing development.

The two men were hunting raccoons Thursday when they stumbled on the first set of prints, which appeared to be of a humanoid foot 15 inches long.

LOCAL LAWMEN who examined the prints said they didn't appear to be obvious hoaxes.

One officer, Mark Pittenger, said he has seen such tracks before, and believes them to have been made by a large, unknown animal that walks erect.

Stories of a giant, hairy ape known variously as "sasquatch" or "bigfoot" have persisted in Northwest legend for more than 100 years.

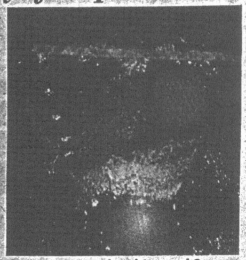

Sasquatch—his mark?

The second set of tracks, purportedly found several hundred yards from the first, are reported to be only about 12 inches long.

"Now we wonder if there could be two of them," said Grove.

BOTH SETS of tracks were found in a densely wooded area near 112th Street and Shaw Road on the edge of Puyallup.

Residents of the area have been unnerved by eerie howls at night. Woodsmen say the howls probably are made by coyotes or timber wolves, but none have been seen.

Grove and Beckman are both employes of Northwest Meats, a Tacoma packing firm.

This article is another such example, containing information that may allow you to search for further information and possibly corroborating witness accounts.

Wild Indian Gets Credit For Gigantic Footprints

SEATTLE—AP—Al Corbett, a Seattle taxidermist, says Bigfoot, the creature whose huge, human like footprints have the natives of the Weitchpec area of Northern California guessing, is an Indian gone wild.

Corbett said he and another taxidermist, Robert Titmus of Anderson, Calif., inspected the tracks 25 miles north of Weitchpec on Saturday and found the prints to be "very large, definitely human, tracks."

16 Inches Long

Corbett reported the clearest print was 16 inches long, five inches across at the heel and seven inches across at the ball of the foot.

A logger in the area, Gerald Crew, last week brought out a plaster cast of a clear footprint. Corbett reported Titmus had furnished Crew with the plaster with which to make the cast.

"The story behind this is that there was a mentally deficient Indian boy who was kept chained by his parents," Corbett said.

Breaks Chains

"When this boy was 17 years old, 28 years ago, he broke the chains and disappeared. The Indians found his clothes but never saw him again. They said he had extremely large feet.

"We talked it over a great deal and figured this man now must be 6 feet, 7 inches to 7 feet, 6 inches tall. We thought he might weigh as much as 400 pounds. He made firm footprints in hard ground.

"Measuring the footprints for a distance of more than 60 feet, we found the average stride was 50 inches. We checked this against the stride of a man 6 feet, 4 inches tall, with long legs, and his stride was 30 inches.

Stride Is 10 Feet

"We were told by people who saw footprints made when this unknown man was running that they were 10 feet apart.

"I know positively this is a human being.

"It seems logical that it is this Indian who disappeared and is living wild. He does his traveling at night. He has not molested anyone. We learned these tracks have been appearing for the past 10 years."

Corbett said Titmus is preparing to set up camera traps in an effort to obtain a photo of Bigfoot.

THE FRESNO BEE

FRESNO, CALIFORNIA,
WEDNESDAY, OCTOBER 8, 1958

I wish to provide a few more examples here, sometimes you may contact the newspaper companies that published the original article, this is best as it may be the closest you can get to the original information such as the following article on "Jacko" the presumably young Sasquatch captured by a railroad crew.

THE CLEVELAND LEADER, MONDAY MORNING, AUGUST 11, 1884.
A WESTERN WHAT IS IT?
A Mysterious Creature in British Columbia.

The village of Yale, B. C., is situated at the head of navigation on Fraser River, ninety miles above New Westminster, which was the capital of British Columbia until it was changed to Victoria. About twenty miles from Yale, on the line of the railroad, is a locality roughly known as "Tunnel No. 4," where the extraordinary occurrence about to be related took place during the early part of the present month.

Notwithstanding the improbability of any amount of prospecting resulting in turning up even the bones of the "missing link," much less in finding an actual living specimen of this much debated being, the actual facts which are related concerning the remarkable appearance near "Tunnel No. 4," would tend to bear out this theory of the subject. At different times during the past two years there has been seen in the hilly country about the settlements a being whose personal appearance is variously described.

One day about a year ago a party of young people from Yale went up on the road as far as Tunnel No. 4, and there, disembarking from the cars, proceeded to spread themselves over the country in the form of a picnic party. The tempting meal had been spread upon the ground, and young men and girls were seated in a circle preparing to enjoy the viands, when there was heard a loud crashing noise above their heads, and in an instant, without further warning there was given by a most fiendish yell—something between the shriek of a hyena and the Indian war whoop—there dropped into the midst of the spread a horrible creature as large as a man, covered with hair from head to foot, with long arms which he brandished about in formidable style, as he vainly tried to extricate himself from the canned fruits, cold meats, jam pots, and oleomargarine into which he had unexpectedly tumbled. This was a "surprise party" for which no intentional preparation had been made, and in a moment there was a stampede.

Tumbling headlong down the hill on whose crest the elaborate meal had been laid, the frightened picknickers so hastened their departure as to be utterly unable to give any coherent description of what had frightened them to the railroad men whose assistance they implored. A party fully armed was at once made up, and the scene of the sudden onslaught was carefully approached. The unwelcome visitor had fled, but before leaving he had plainly helped himself to everything that took his fancy, and that seemed to have been guided by nothing but the opportunity. If he were a human creature and had eaten what was certainly gone, selected from every imaginable article of food, his remains would undoubtedly be found in a few hours. No idiot Indian or other kind of man could possibly have eaten such a mixture and live.

But if such was the case, the most careful search failed to result in finding the body, and after a protracted search, which lasted, after a desultory fashion, for several weeks, the idea of his having died of indigestion or gout was reluctantly abandoned. One fact which was demonstrated by the circumstance of this visitation caused the believers in the Indian theory to be very deeply shaken in their convictions. This was that he had fallen from an overhanging limb of a tree, carrying a large piece with him, and the size of the limb was a good indication that the creature must be as heavy as an ordinary sized man, and hardly an Indian, as they do not usually climb trees. A few months later another view of this strange being was had by some workmen on the railroad, but, though they gave chase, they were not able to come up with him. He was not seen again until about three weeks ago, when he was not only seen, but caught. The spot where he was discovered was a series of bluffs, deemed inaccessible. A train was running from Lytton to Yale, when the engineer saw what he supposed to be a man lying close to the track. He whistled down brakes, but just as the train stopped the object sprang to its feet, and in an instant the object was climbing the side of the precipitous declivity with the greatest ease. The conductor, brakemen, express messenger, and a number of passengers at once gave chase, and after some perilous climbing succeeded in corralling the creature on an overhanging shelf of rock from which he could neither ascend nor descend. The ingenious, though rather cruel, method was now adopted for securing him, of dropping a piece of stone from above, which, falling on his head, stunned him, and he fell insensible.

The bell rope was now procured, and, after some expert climbing, he was reached, tied, and lowered gradually down to the foot of the cliff. He was placed in the baggage car and successfully transported to Yale, when it was found that he had recovered from his insensibility, and was tractable and docile. One of the men in the railroad machine shop assumed the care of him, named him Jacko, and very soon made his friendly acquaintance. And even then, and up to the present time, it has not been satisfactorily ascertained to what race the new discovery belongs. He is of the gorilla type, but not definitely enough to be declared a gorilla, which is, moreover, a creature unknown to the latitude of British Columbia—while there has been no menagerie there to introduce even a monkey. He is about 4 feet 7 inches in height, and weighs 127 pounds. His entire body, except his hands and feet, is covered with black, glossy hair about one inch in length, but his forearm is much longer than that of a man, and so strong that he will break a stick—by wrenching or twisting it—so large that no man could possibly accomplish this feat. He makes a noise, half bark and half growl, but is generally quiet. His favorite food is berries, and he drinks fresh milk with evident relish. His captor intends taking him to London for exhibition. Then his exact position in natural history will probably be discovered.

On the following page is the same article but published in Ohio:

In conducting your research I would also recommend some of the early books written on the subject of Bigfoot, they contain information that include witness accounts, locations, witness names which may be useful. Ivan Sanderson's book from the early 1960's is a good one, "Abominable Snowmen Legend Come to Life", while Sanderson did discuss the Yeti of the Himalayan mountains a great deal he also covered the Sasquatch of North America and the book is well worth having especially for anyone new to the topic and wanting foundational knowledge.

Often today people are too caught up in what's happening currently, but ignoring the vast wealth of information from these early sources risks missing out much valuable information.

This is the current version but well worth having.

Another author and pioneer of the subject of Bigfoot is John Green, Green wrote three very good magazine-style books from 1968 to 1973, the first is "On the Track of the Sasquatch"

These books have seen a number of changes throughout the years since first published but contain essentially the same information and my opinion is they are essential for anyone just becoming involved in the subject.

The next one published by Green was "Year of the Sasquatch"

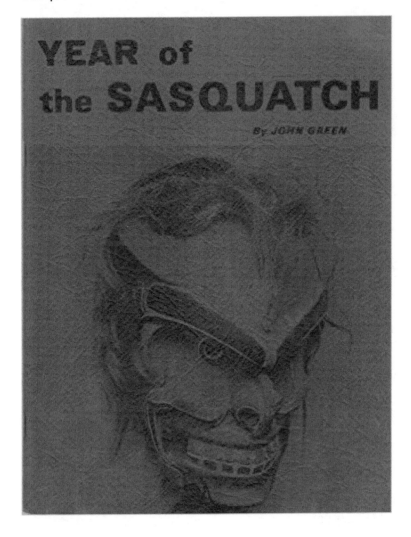

The third book John Green published was not as popular as his first two; however it contains more references and is in my opinion the best of the three for use as a reference starting point for beginning your search. That book was titled "The Sasquatch File"

There are other books I would recommend, "Sasquatch" by Don Hunter with Rene Dahinden is good, but contains essentially the same information as John Green's books.

There was also a book titled "Bigfoot" by anthropologist John Napier that is very good.

And of course, my first book "Notes From the Field, Tracking North America's Sasquatch" contains useful information that may assist you.

All these books have information that may be useful to you, depending on your location and places where historically people have encountered these creatures and in conjunction with newspaper articles you will have more information to provide you with an informed decision as to where you may to start.

All of this information is intended to provide you with a starting point, and if there is not a great deal of historical information in your region but do not get disappointed. As long as there has been some witness testimony of seeing these creatures, it could be that most were never reported and you can still use what's available to make a choice of where to begin searching.

The next thing I would advise is to get maps of the area you have chosen. Maps are updated on a regular basis, which is a good thing since roads and structures change over time. One problem with updates to maps however, are that names of roads and places can change as well.

What I recommend are obtaining older maps of areas you choose to look in, if you are basing a search on old articles or information from some of the books I have recommended then names of many locations may have changed and are no longer found on newer maps. One example is a book titles David Thompsons Narrative. Thompson worked for the Hudson Bay company and in 1847 had desired to go to Mount Saint Helens in southern Washington, but none of the native people's there would take him there as they greatly feared the "cannibals" that were said to inhabit the region.

This is the quote from Thompson:

"March 27, 1847":
"When we arrived at the mouth of the Kattlepoutal River, 26

miles from Vancouver, I stopped to make a sketch of the volcano, Mt. St. Helens, distant I suppose, about 30 or 40 miles. This mountain has never been visited by either whites or Indians; the latter assert that it is inhabited by a race of beings of a different species, who are cannibals, and who they hold in great dread...these superstitions are taken from a man they say went in to the mountains with another, and escaped the fate of his companion, who was eaten by the 'skookums', or 'evil genii'. I offered a considerable bribe to any Indian who would accompany me in its exploration but could not find one hardly enough to venture there".

Artist Paul Kane also mentioned this in writing. The following is a bit of the historical information on the river:

Early Lewis River...

> In 1792 Lieutenant Broughton of the Captain George Vancouver Expedition passed by the Lewis River on October 28, 1792, and named the Lewis River "Rushleigh's River".
>> "... At point Warrior the river is divided into three branches; the middle one was the largest, about a quarter of a mile wide, and was considered as the main branch; the next most capacious took an easterly directions, and seemed extensive, to this the name of Rushleigh's River was given; and the other that stretched to the S. S. W. was distinguished by the name of Call's River. ..." [Vancouver, October 28, 1792]
>
> Warrior Point is the downstream tip of Sauvie Island and the "river" mentioned is the Columbia River. The three branches are "Call's River", today's Multnomah Channel, the Columbia, and "Rushleigh's River", today's Lewis

River.

Lewis and Clark passed the Lewis River on November 5, 1805, but did not make mention of it. On their return in March 1806 the Indians inform the men of the river which they call the *Chah-wah-na-hi-ooks* (see information presented above).

When the artist Paul Kane wrote about the Lewis River on March 26, 1847, he called the river the "Kattlepoutal River".

> "... When we arrived at the mouth of the Kattlepoutal River, twenty-six miles from Fort Vancouver, I stopped to make a sketch of the volcano, Mount St. Helen's, distant, I suppose, about thirty or forty miles. [Paul Kane, 1859, "Wanderings of an Artist among the Indians of North America", London]

In 1853 the railroad mapped the North Fork Lewis River as "Cathlapootle River".

Another early name for the Lewis River was the "Washington River".

An 1854 Washington Territory cadastral survey (tax survey) for T4N R1W has the Lewis River labelled the "Catapoodle R.". The State of Oregon cadastral survey for the same year has the Lewis as the "Cadapoodle River". Washington Territory's 1862 cadastral survey matches Oregon with the Lewis River being the "Cadapoodle River".

An article in the "Pioneer and Democrat" newspaper (August 5, 1854, p.3) called the Lewis River the

"Cathlapoodle River".

> "... Gold on Cathlapoodle River. --- We learn from Mr. Huff, that valuable mines have been discovered on the Cathlapoodle river, some 30 or 40 miles above its mouth. Large quantities of gold, silver, and rich iron ore, have been found on this river. The Cathlapoodle takes its rise at Mt. St. Helens, and empties into the Columbia at the lower end of Sauvé's Island. It is also reported that there are rich mines in the vicinity of Mt. St. Helens.-- *Times*

In 1866 Lincoln, one of the first settlements along the Lewis River was founded. This small trading post and post office were located at the mouth of Lockwood Creek, named after Reuben Lockwood who settled in the area.

In 1881 <u>Woodland</u> was established on the Lewis River four miles upstream of its confluence with the Columbia.

The 1881 U.S. Coast and Geodetic Survey's Chart No.5, "Kalama to Fales Landing", lists the Lewis as the "Lewis River".

In 1929 the U.S. Board of Geographic Names made official the name "Lewis River".

As you can see digging into the regions history a little can yield valuable information linking places where the Sasquatch had been noted in the past to names of locations that had been re-named may certainly help you understand the current areas connected to them.

Metskers maps are a real asset in this quest for clarification of old names to new ones, doing an online search for Metskers maps works well and they are very helpful to areas you may be interested in searching, they will often contain old names and when compared with contemporary maps you can glean information using old original accounts and place you at those locations.

If you cannot find maps with older information, you may try contacting your county clerk's office and asking about older names that no longer appear on current maps.

One very good resource today is Google earth, once you have compiled plenty of historical information you can use Google earth to mark regions with your newly acquired data. Here is an example of such a use.

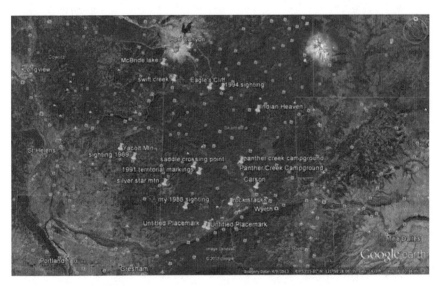

Once you have established a historical pattern in your chosen region, you may want to create this sort of mapping of activity year by year beginning from your earliest historical records of the creature's activities in your region.

Over time you may find cyclical patterns of activity, this can help you anticipate future areas of activity. The following map was created by the Jevning Research Group team in Utah:

Mapping results of your research is very helpful, and allows you to narrow your searches to particular areas.

The next step in choosing your search area is to research what wildlife inhabits your area; you can search your state website on the fish and game section and familiarize yourself on the various kinds of animals that live there. It will be helpful to have some understanding of feeding habits of wildlife, population sizes and movement patterns.

This where you may choose to utilize my suggestion of the National Audubon Society book on mammals I recommended in volume one.

You should also have some familiarity with the various kinds of vegetation and tree's that grow in your region, having a basic understanding of the flora and fauna can aid in understanding the Sasquatches movements as they live and feed in these regions also, and will take advantage of many of the same food sources as other creatures.

Another item you may wish to familiarize yourself with is the available water sources, as all wildlife will need these, and Sasquatch is no different.

One last item that has a big impact on wildlife and in particular the Sasquatch is human population and impacts on wilderness areas. The Sasquatch will actively keep away from human activity, however on occasion will venture near human habitation areas scavenging or foraging for an easy meal but we will discuss this in another volume.

Over time, as you apply the information you have collected to maps, you may see patterns of activity emerge through time; you will need to adjust the encroachment of human population to these calculations as the Sasquatches will have adjusted their movement patterns as well.

One clue when you research through historical information, are the behaviors toward witnesses in those accounts. This may provide some helpful information on how Sasquatch adjustments to human encroachments alter where they have moved. If encounters were most often violent in nature or aggressive then the distance from human populations may be greater and likewise if less aggressive behaviors were observed then distances may be less. One thing is any given group of creature's temperament and behaviors in response to human presence will be different so use this information cautiously as it may not reflect the current behavioral situation in your region.

If possible, Native Americans in your region may be willing to also provide you with some insight historically. Often however most Native peoples do not wish to share what they know with "outsiders" but you may be lucky and either is of Native ancestry and have family connections that me be willing to share tribal knowledge with you or have friends who are Native Americans and willing to tell you some historical information. Can also go online there are Native websites with stories and myths.

These things I have suggested will help you establish where you should begin your field searches, done properly you should have some luck locating evidence of the presence of these creatures in the areas you have chosen.

About the Author

William Jevning has been a field investigator and researcher of the creatures known as Sasquatch since 1972. Previous books are Notes From the Field, Tracking North America's Sasquatch, Haunted Valley and In Search of the Unknown.

Made in the USA
Columbia, SC
12 November 2023